BIG
Kids' First
BIBLE

This book belongs to:

Zach

It was given to me by:

Milton Baptist Toddler Group

On:

20th March 2024

Contents

The Very Beginning of Everything ··········· 6
God Makes the Sun, Moon, and Stars ······· 8
God Creates Animals ···························· 10
The First People ································· 12
The Garden of Eden ···························· 14
A Fresh Beginning ······························ 16
God Calls Abraham ····························· 18
God Gives Abraham a Son ···················· 20
Joseph Forgives His Brothers ················· 22
Moses is Pulled from the River ··············· 24
A New Family for Ruth and Naomi ·········· 26
God Talks to Samuel ··························· 28
David is Chosen as King ······················· 30
David Defeats Goliath ························· 32
David's Best Friend ····························· 34
David Writes Songs of Praise ················· 36
God is Our Shepherd ··························· 38
God's Word is Our Light ······················· 40
Solomon Asks for Wisdom ···················· 42
The Greatest Love Song Ever ················· 44
Esther Saves Her People ······················· 46
The Fiery Furnace ······························· 48
Daniel in the Lions' Den ······················· 50
Jonah Runs from God ·························· 52

God's Son is Here! · 54
Wise Men Visit Jesus · 56
"Follow Me!" · 58
"Get Up and Walk!" · 60
Shine Like a Bright Light · 62
"Do Not Worry!" · 64
"Young Man, Get Up!" · 66
Jesus Calms the Storm · 68
Jairus' Daughter Comes Back to Life · 70
"Because of Your Faith, be Healed!" · 72
A Boy Shares His Food · 74
"Let the Children Come to Me!" · 76
Zacchaeus is Changed · 78
Jesus Rides into Jerusalem · 80
The Praise of Children · 82
Jesus Dies on a Cross · 84
Jesus is Buried · 86
Jesus Defeats Death · 88
"I am with You Always!" · 90
Jesus Returns to Heaven · 92
God's Great Salvation Plan · 94

The Very Beginning of Everything
Genesis 1:1–13

Back at the very beginning, God created the world! He simply spoke, and everything came into being. He made light and darkness, the sky, the oceans, and the land, but He wasn't done yet. God filled the land with plants of all shapes and sizes, from huge trees to tiny flowers.

God Makes the Sun, Moon, and Stars

Genesis 1:14–19

God created the world, but He also made the universe! He created the sun to give light to our day, and the moon for a night-light. He made the stars and put them all in place. God gave us these heavenly bodies to tell the time and keep track of the seasons—He thinks of everything!

God Creates Animals

Genesis 1:20–25

God didn't just make an empty world—He wanted to fill it with life! God made animals to swim in the water, to fly in the sky, and to walk on the land. All the creatures that we see, from the biggest to the smallest, God made them all.

The First People

Genesis 1:26-31; 2:1–25

God wanted someone who could love Him and take care of the world. He created a man in His image, made him out of dust, and breathed life into him. God made a woman from the man's rib to be his partner, so he wouldn't be alone. These first humans lived together with God; they were very happy.

The Garden of Eden

Genesis 3

Adam and Eve lived in a perfect garden with God—it was wonderful! God had only one rule: do not eat the fruit of a certain tree. One day, a snake convinced Adam and Eve to disobey God and eat anyway. Because they had sinned, God sent Adam and Eve out of the garden.

A Fresh Beginning

Genesis 8–9:17

The Earth was soon full of evil people who sinned all the time. God was so upset that He decided to destroy everything with a flood and start anew. He told Noah, the only good man left, to build a huge boat to keep his family and the animals safe. After the waters dried up, God promised never to flood the whole world again.

God Calls Abraham

Genesis 12:1–3

Many years later, God spoke to a man named Abraham and told him to go to a faraway country. God promised to bless Abraham and make his family into a great nation. Not only that, but God promised that everyone on earth would be blessed through Abraham and his family. Abraham believed God and followed Him.

God Gives Abraham a Son

Genesis 21:1–7

God promised to make Abraham the father of many nations, but he didn't have any children. Abraham and his wife Sarah were too old to have children any more. When God promised to give them a son, Sarah laughed because she thought it was impossible. Nothing is impossible for God, and He kept His promise. Abraham and Sarah named their son Isaac, which means laughter.

Joseph Forgives His Brothers

Genesis 39–45

Abraham's grandson Jacob had twelve sons. He loved his son Joseph the most, and Joseph's brothers were so jealous that they sold him as a slave. God used Joseph's troubles for good, helping him save Egypt from a terrible famine. When Joseph's brothers came to Egypt for food, he forgave them for what they had done to him.

Moses is Pulled from the River
Exodus 2:1–10

Joseph's family, the Israelites, were slaves in Egypt for a long time. Pharaoh ordered that all Israelite boy babies should be killed. Moses' mother hid him from Pharaoh and put him in the river in a floating basket. The princess took Moses from the water and raised him as her own son. God used Moses to lead the Israelites out of Egypt to a land of their very own.

A New Family for Ruth and Naomi

Ruth 1–4

An Israelite woman named Naomi lived in a country called Moab, where she lost both of her sons and her husband. Naomi's daughter-in-law Ruth came back with her to Israel to take care of her. In Israel, Ruth met a man named Boaz who provided food for her and Naomi. Boaz married Ruth and they had a baby boy. God had given Ruth and Naomi a new family!

God Talks to Samuel

1 Samuel 3:1–11

A boy named Samuel lived at the place where everyone came to worship God. One night, God called to Samuel while he was sleeping. Samuel thought it was Eli the priest, but Eli said, "God is calling you." The next time God called Samuel, he said, "Speak, God! I am your servant, and I am listening." God told Samuel that He would use him as a leader and prophet for Israel, to help them follow God's will.

David is Chosen as King

1 Samuel 16:1–13

God sent Samuel to Bethlehem to choose a new king for Israel, because the current king had disobeyed Him. Samuel came to the family of a man named Jesse, and talked with each of his sons. God didn't choose any of the older boys to be king. Instead, God chose David, the youngest, who was in the fields watching his father's sheep.

David Defeats Goliath

1 Samuel 17:1–51

The Israelites were fighting their enemies, the Philistines. A huge giant named Goliath threatened the Israelite army, and no one was brave enough to fight him. David heard about Goliath and volunteered to fight the giant. God was with David, and he beat Goliath with only a sling and a stone.

David's Best Friend

1 Samuel 18:1–4

Saul was the king before David, and his son Jonathan became best friends with David. They were so close that they were like brothers. Jonathan even shared his royal clothes and weapons with his friend David. When King Saul wanted to try to kill David, Jonathan warned him so he could get away.

David Writes Songs of Praise

2 Samuel 22; Psalm 18

David loved to sing praises to God. He wrote many songs of worship, thanking God for saving him from his enemies and taking care of him. David also wrote songs about how faithful God is and how good his words are. David praised God all the time for the wonderful things He had done. Even after David became king of Israel, he kept writing and singing songs of praise to God!

God is Our Shepherd

Psalm 23

One of David's songs compares God to a shepherd. This song talks about how God guides and protects us, even when things are scary. David also talks about how God provides for our needs. Because God is our shepherd, He gives us goodness and love all our lives, and we will live with Him for ever.

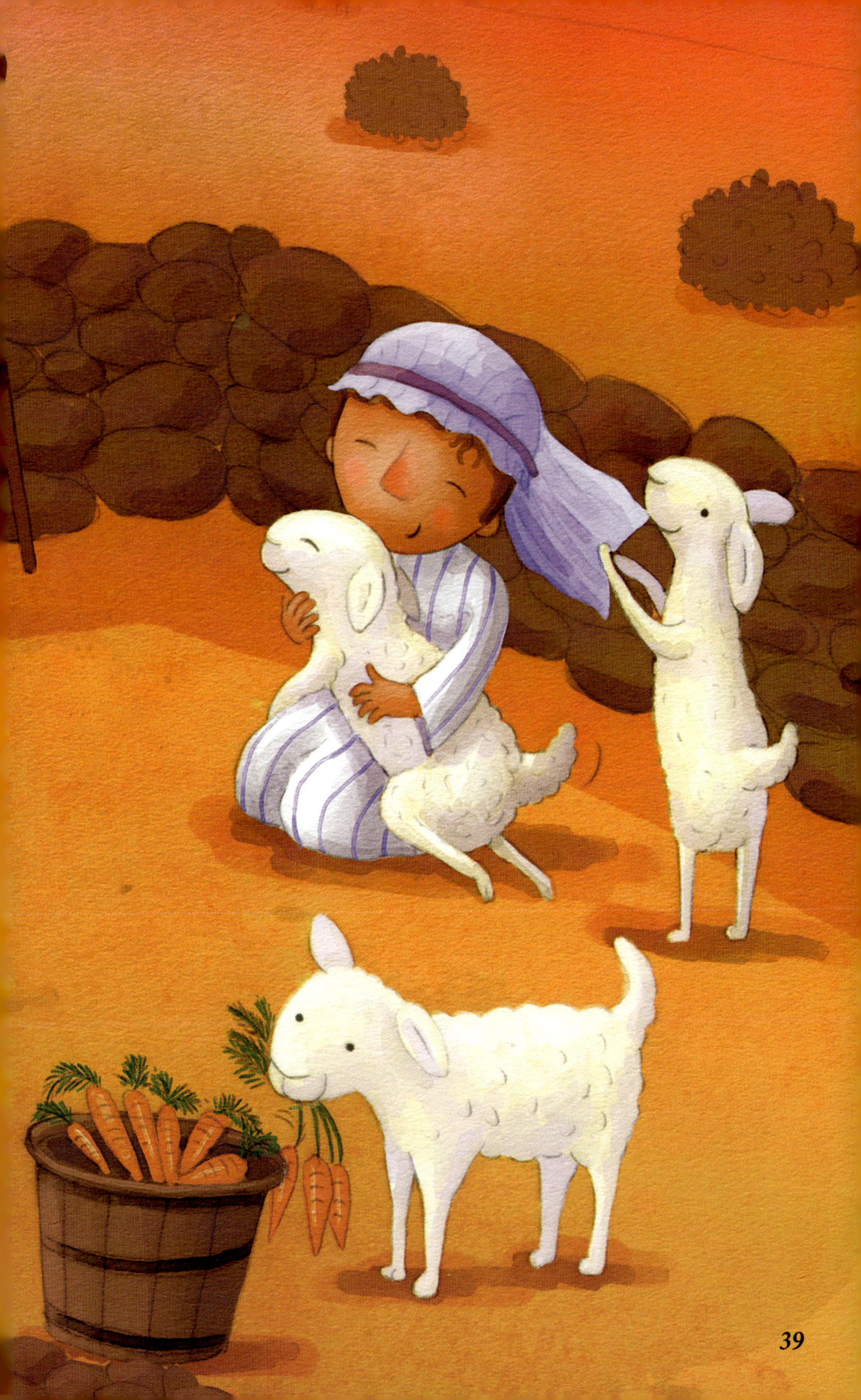

God's Word is Our Light

Psalm 119:105

David's longest song is all about God's word and how much he loves it. In that song, David says,
"Your word is a lamp
that lights my path
wherever I walk."
God gave us His word, the Bible, so we can know Him and how much He loves us.

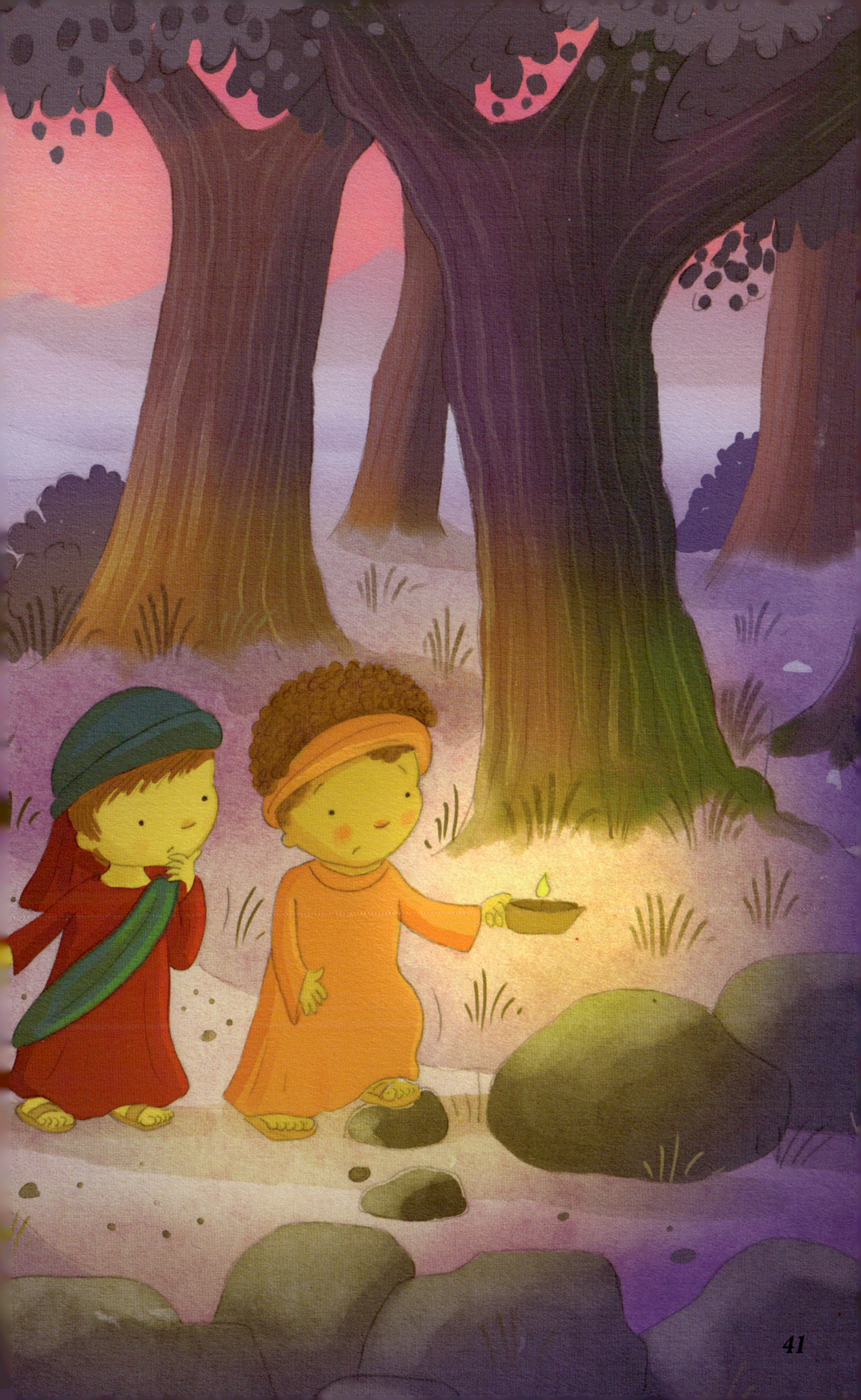

Solomon Asks for Wisdom

1 Kings 3:5–15

David's son Solomon became king after him. God appeared to Solomon in a dream and told him to ask for whatever he wanted. Solomon asked God for the wisdom to rule Israel well. God was happy that Solomon asked for wisdom, and He made him the wisest man who ever lived.

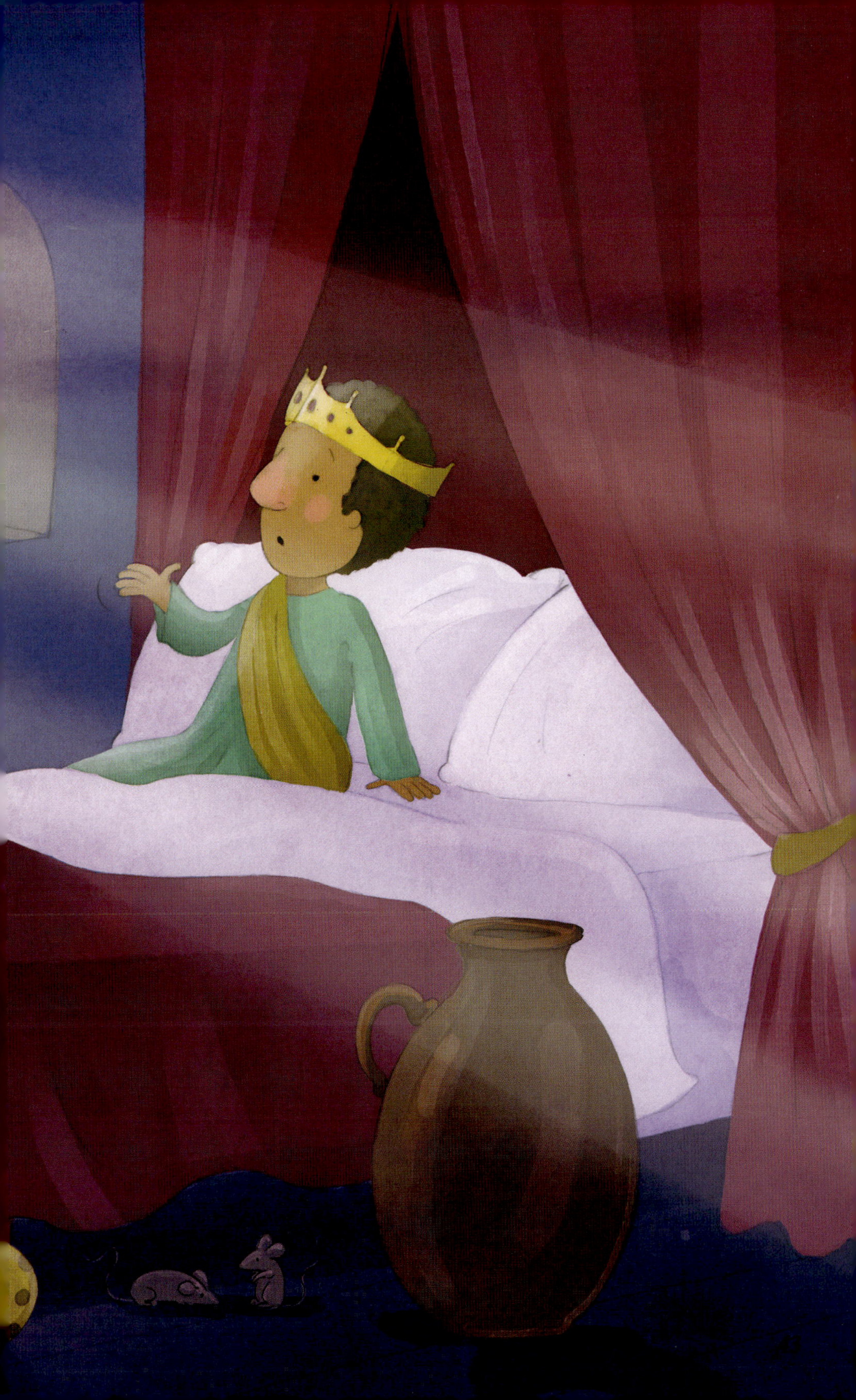

The Greatest Love Song Ever

Song of Songs 1–8

Solomon loved his wife so much that he wrote a song all about how much he loved her. This song is a wonderful love story, but it is also a picture of God's love for us. God loves us even more than Solomon loved his wife. When we know how much God loves us, we can't help but love Him back!

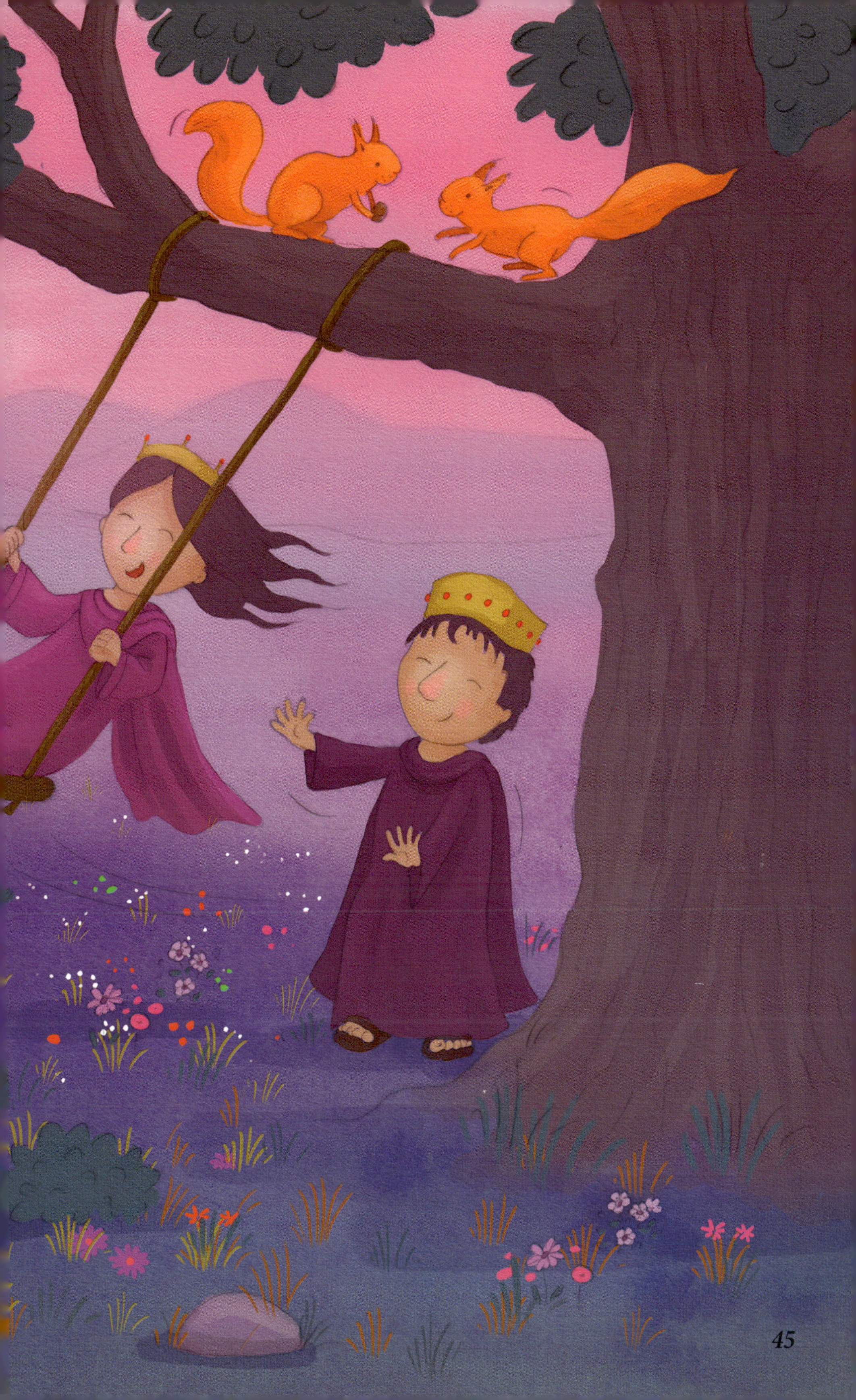

Esther Saves Her People

Esther 2–8

A young Israelite woman named Esther was chosen as the new queen of Persia. An evil man named Haman was plotting to kill the Israelites, but God had a different plan. Esther went before the king, even though it was dangerous, and told him about the plot. The king listened to Esther and saved the Israelites.

47

The Fiery Furnace
Daniel 3

King Nebuchadnezzar of Babylon made a huge golden statue and ordered everyone to worship it. Three young Israelites refused to worship the statue, so Nebuchadnezzar got angry and threw them into a blazing furnace. The fire didn't kill them; instead, God appeared with them and protected them. Nebuchadnezzar praised the God of Israel after seeing this miracle.

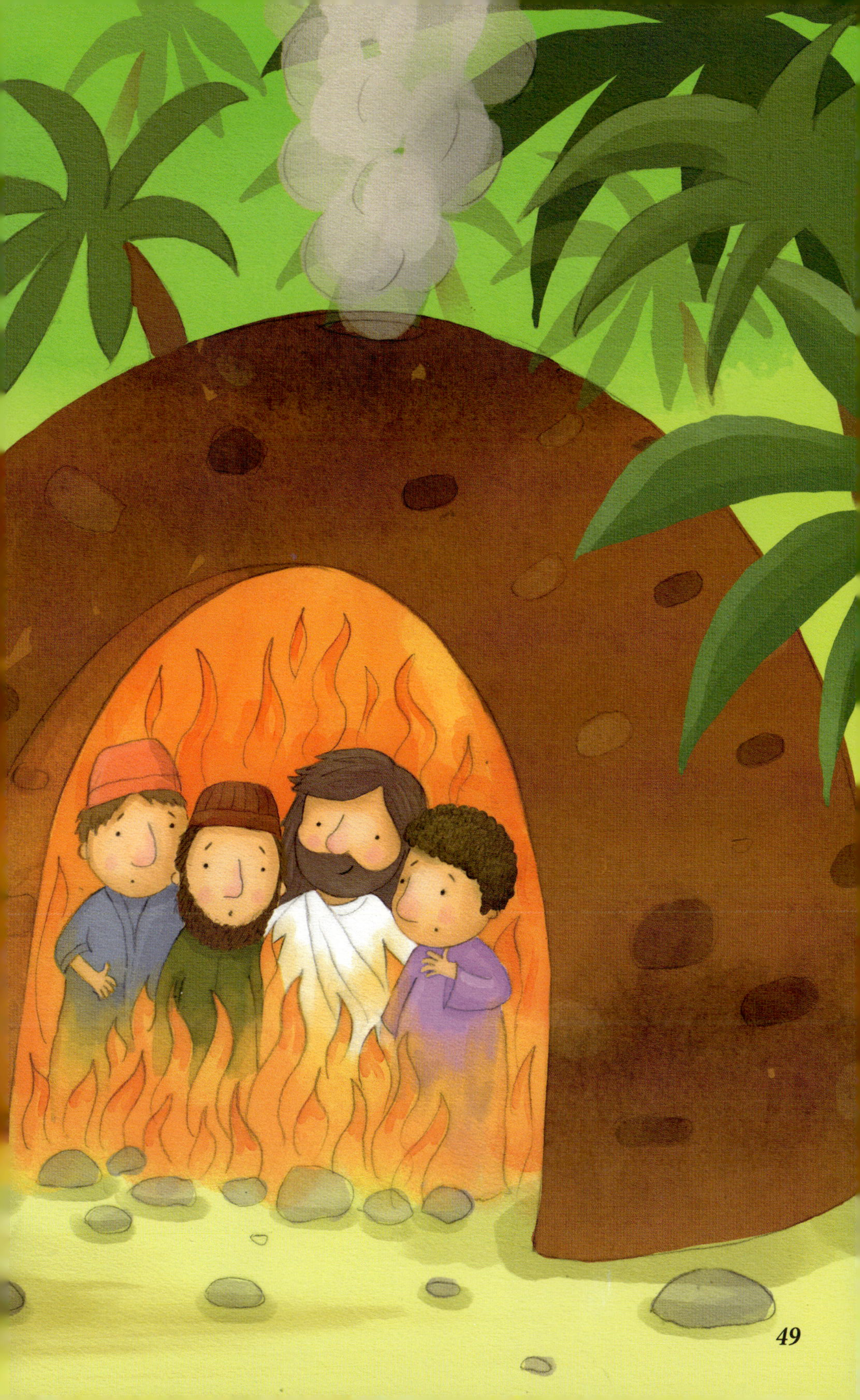

Daniel in the Lions' Den

Daniel 6

Daniel was a trusted helper of the king, and the king's other helpers became jealous. They had the king pass a law making it illegal to pray to anyone but him. When Daniel kept praying to God, the king had him thrown into a pit full of hungry lions. God protected Daniel, and the lions didn't touch him.

51

Jonah Runs from God

Jonah 1–4

Jonah was a prophet who told people what God said. God told him to go preach to the Ninevites. Jonah didn't like the Ninevites, so he ran away on a boat instead. The sailors threw Jonah overboard because of a storm, and he was swallowed by a big fish. The fish spat Jonah out by Nineveh, and when he finally preached to them, they turned to God.

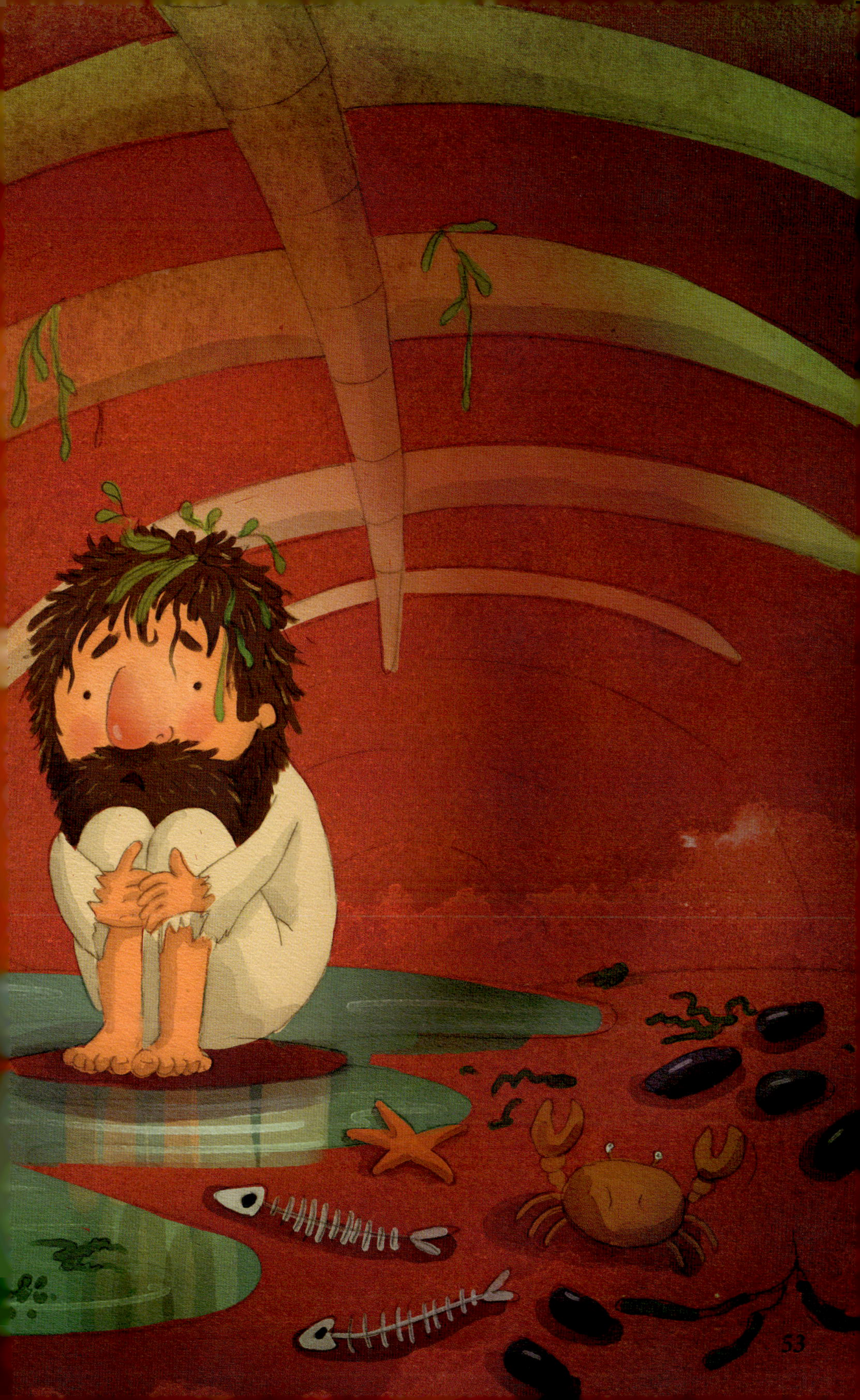

God's Son is Here!

Luke 2:1–7

Many years had passed when an angel appeared to a girl named Mary, telling her that she would have God's son. Mary and her fiancé Joseph travelled to Bethlehem, but there were no spare rooms available, so they stayed in a stable. While they were there, Mary had her baby. She named Him Jesus and laid Him in a manger.

55

Wise Men Visit Jesus

Matthew 2:1–12

When Jesus was born, wise men from the east saw a bright star appear in the sky. They followed that star, and it led them to Bethlehem where Jesus was. The wise men worshipped Jesus and gave Him presents of gold, perfume and oil. They were so happy to meet God's son!

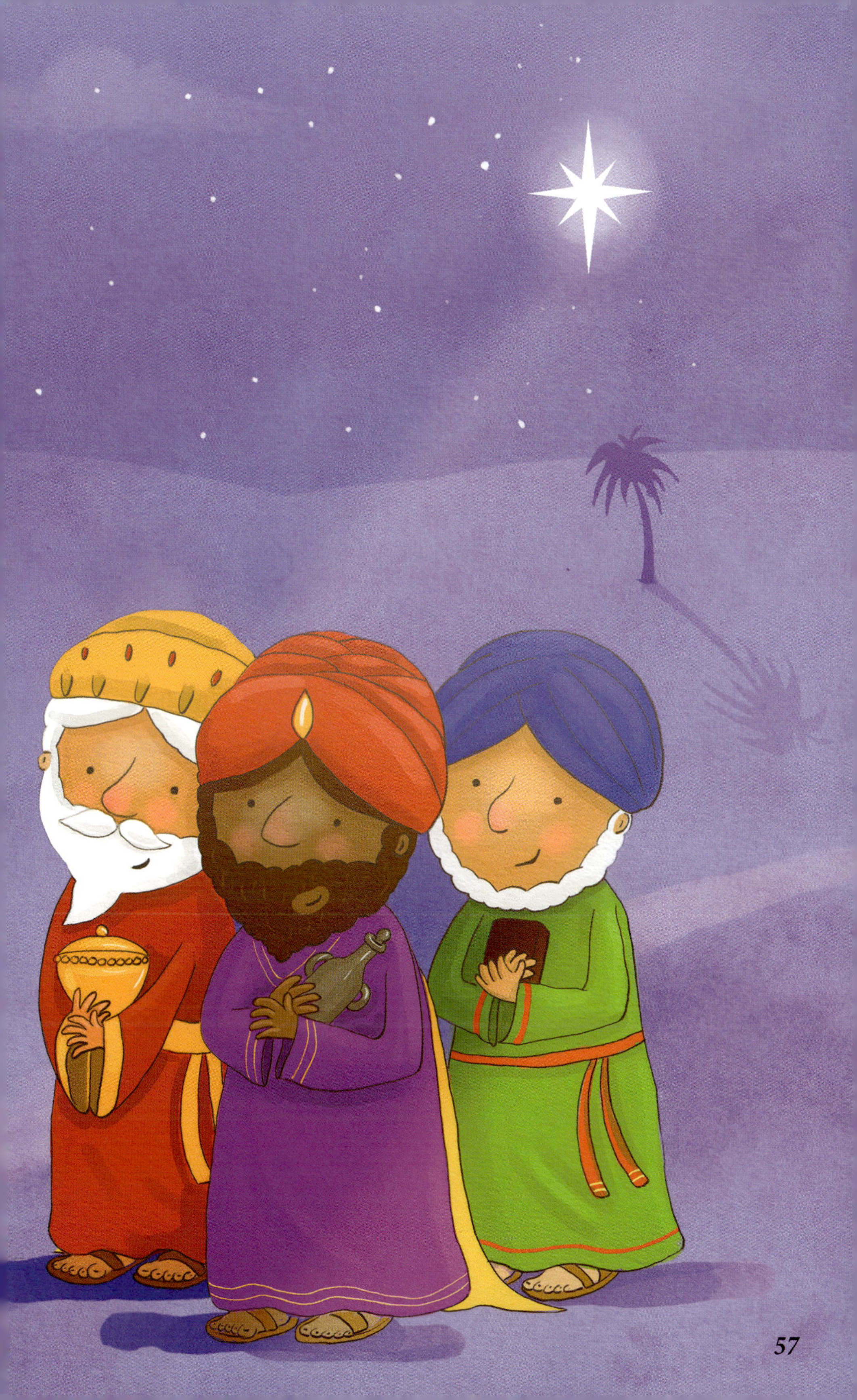

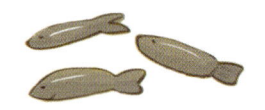

"Follow Me!"

Mark 1:16-20; Luke 5:1–11

Jesus was walking along the Sea of Galilee when He saw some fishermen. They had not caught any fish that day, but He told them to go out and let down their nets. The men were surprised when they caught so many fish that their boats couldn't hold them all! "Follow me," Jesus said. So they left their boats and followed Him.

59

"Get Up and Walk!"

Matthew 9:1–8; Luke 5:17–26

Some people wanted to bring their paralysed friend to see Jesus. There were so many people in the house that they had to lower him down through the roof. When Jesus saw the man, He said, "Your sins are forgiven. Get up and walk!" The man got up and carried his mat home with him—Jesus had healed him!

61

Shine Like a Bright Light

Matthew 5:14–16

Jesus was talking to His followers, and He told them, "You are the light of the world. People don't hide lights under bowls, so don't hide your light either. Let the good things you do be like a light shining for others to see. That way, when they see them, they will praise God in heaven."

63

"Do Not Worry!"

Matthew 6:25–34

Another time when Jesus was teaching His followers, He said, "Do not worry about food or clothes—what you will eat or what you will wear. God takes care of birds and flowers, and they don't worry about those things. You are worth much more than birds or flowers. God will take care of you, too. He knows what you need, so don't worry."

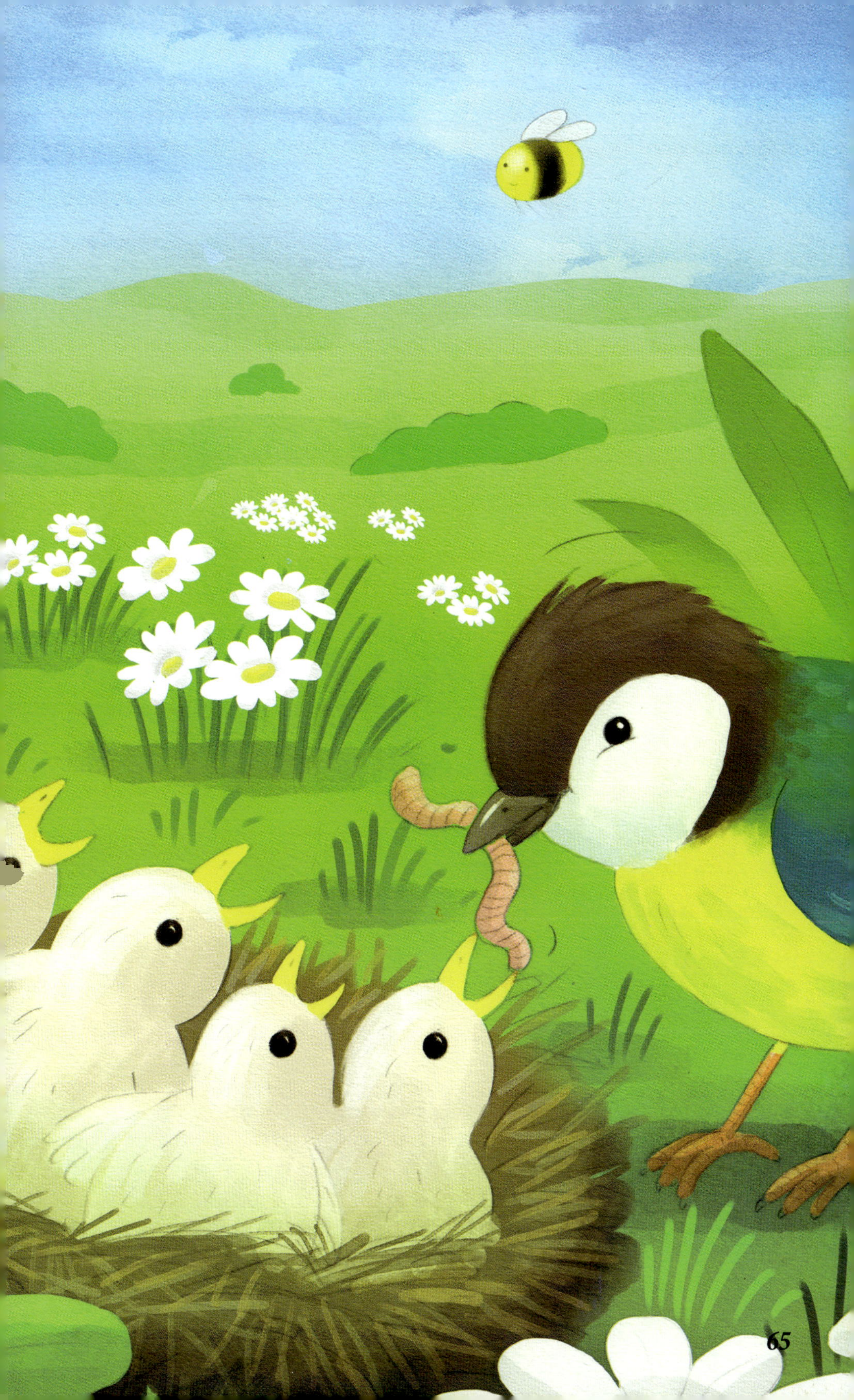

"Young Man, Get Up!"
Luke 7:11–17

Jesus was passing a town when He saw a funeral going on. A woman had lost her only son, and she was crying. Jesus went over and told her not to cry. He said, "Young man, get up!" and the woman's son came back to life! Everyone was amazed and believed in Jesus.

67

Jesus Calms the Storm

Matthew 8:23–27; Mark 4:35–41

One time Jesus was in a boat with His closest followers. A huge storm came up and Jesus' friends thought they were going to sink. Jesus stood up and told the wind and waves to be quiet—and they were! Everyone was amazed at how the storm obeyed Jesus.

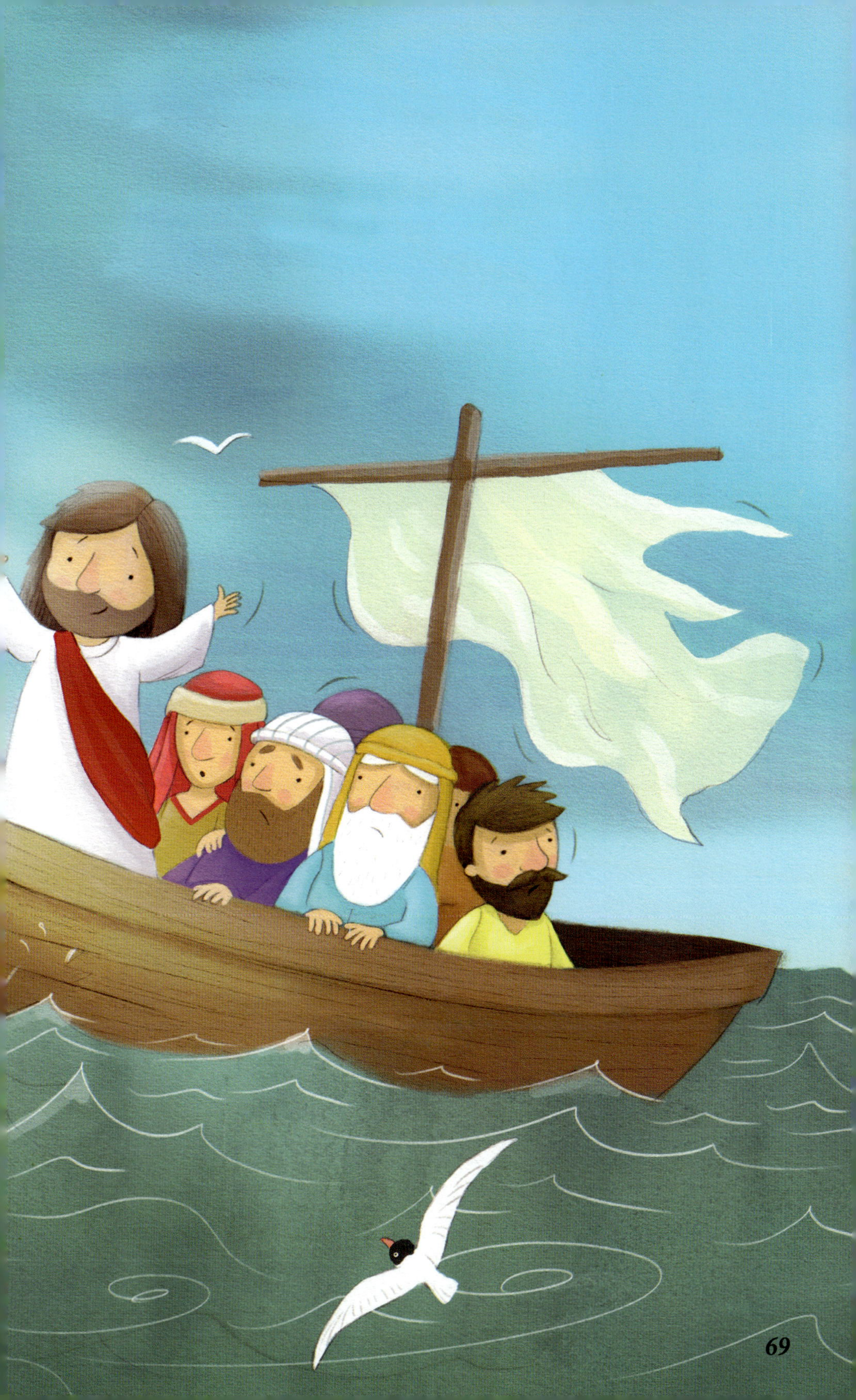

Jairus' Daughter Comes Back to Life

Mark 5:21–43; Luke 8:40–56

A man named Jairus had a daughter who was very ill. Jairus asked Jesus to come and heal his daughter, but before they got back to his house, she died. Jesus told Jairus not to be afraid, but to believe. He took the girl's hand and said, "Get up!" and she came back to life!

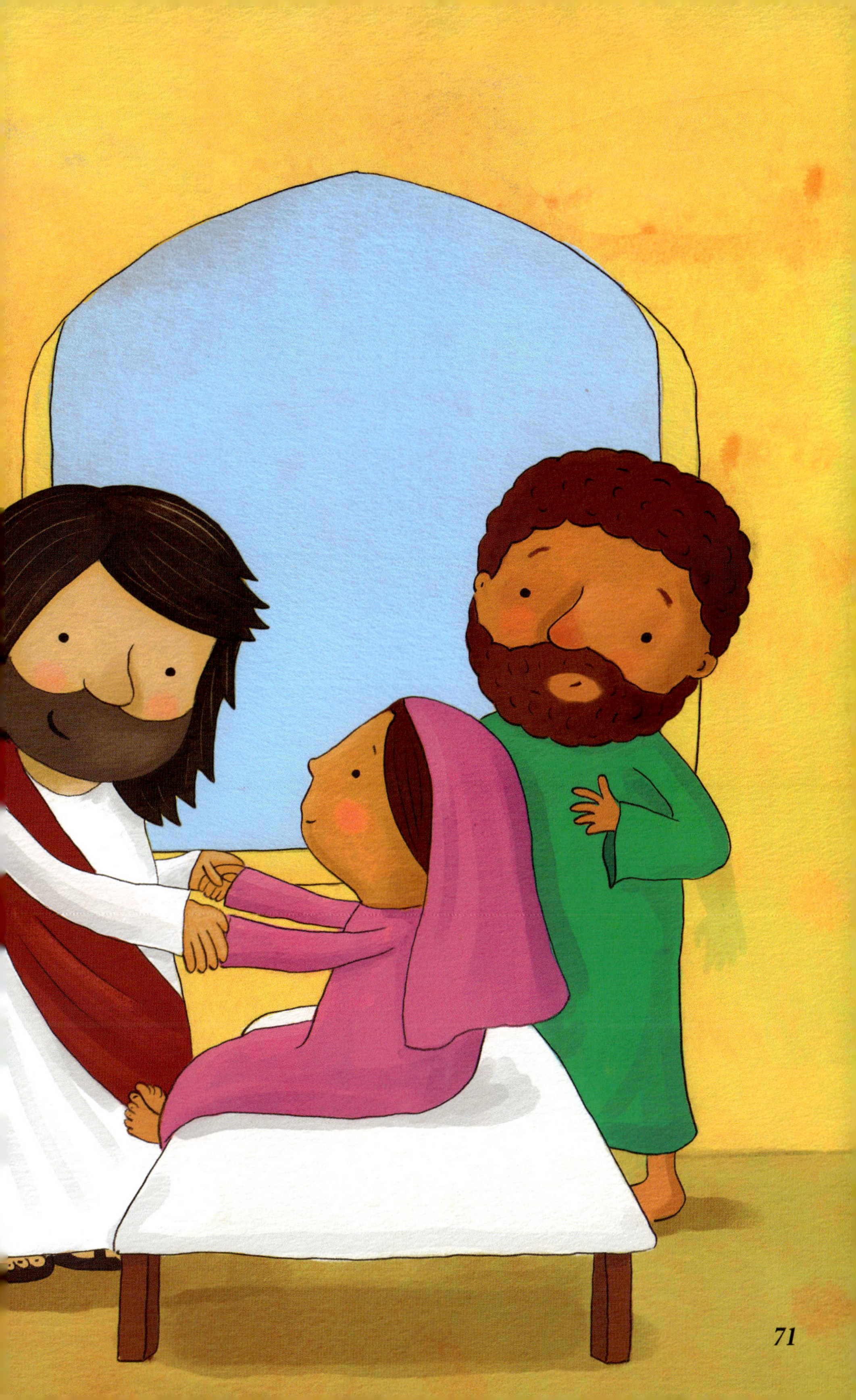

"Because of Your Faith, be Healed!"

Matthew 9:27–31

Two blind men followed Jesus and said, "Have mercy on us!" Jesus asked them if they believed He could heal them. "Yes, Lord," they said.

Jesus touched their eyes and said, "Because of your faith, be healed." Right away, they could see again! They were so excited that they told everyone what Jesus had done for them.

73

A Boy Shares His Food

Matthew 14:13–21; John 6:1–15

A huge crowd of people came to hear Jesus teach. At dinner time everyone was hungry, but almost no one had brought any food. A boy gave Jesus his basket with some bread and fish. Jesus thanked God for the food and started sharing it with everyone. They all had plenty to eat, and there were even leftovers!

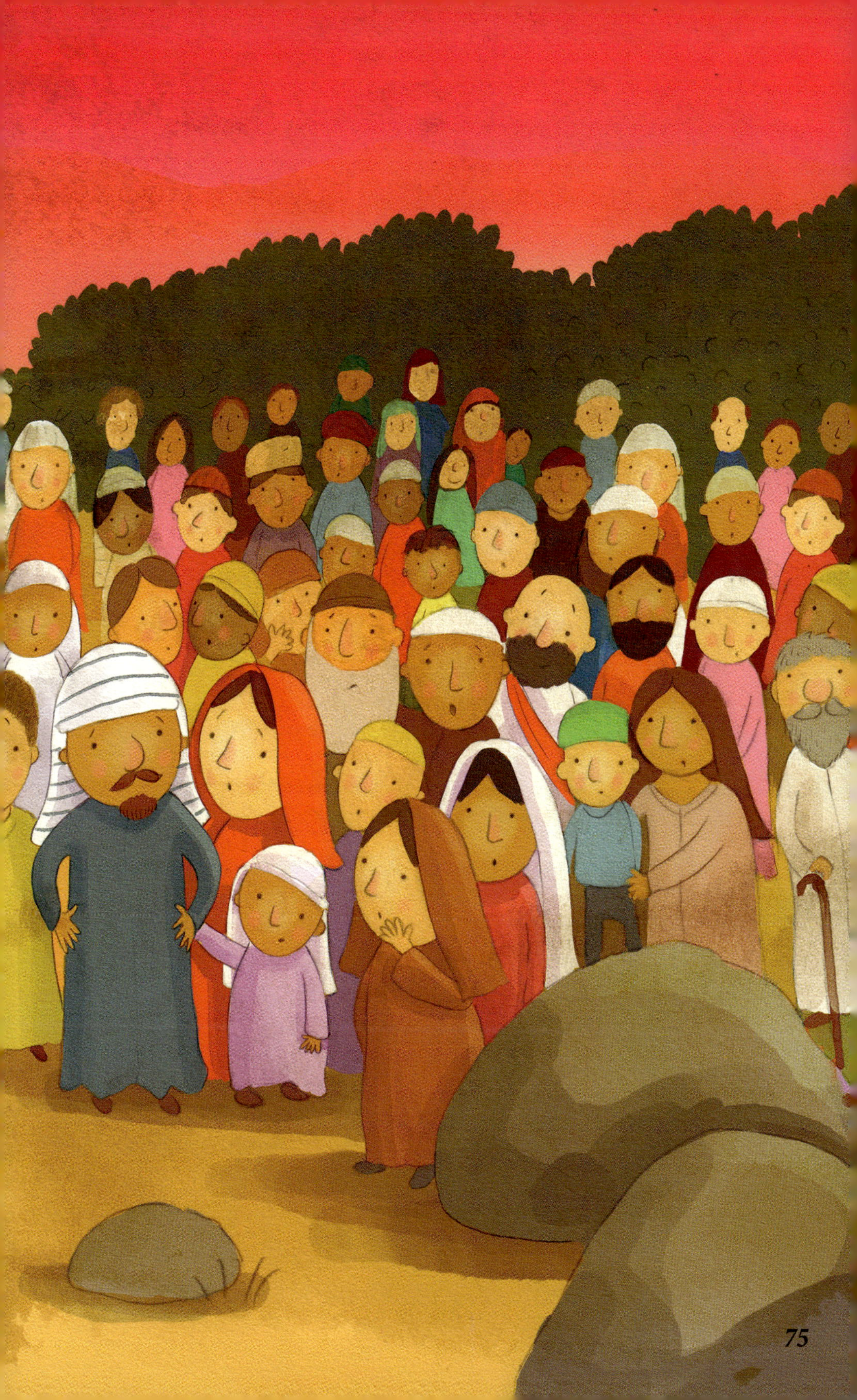

"Let the Children Come to Me!"

Mark 10:13–16; Luke 18:15–17

Some parents wanted to bring their children to see Jesus so He could bless them. Jesus' followers thought He was too important for the children, and tried to shoo them away. Jesus told them to let the children come to Him. "My kingdom belongs to people like these children," He said.

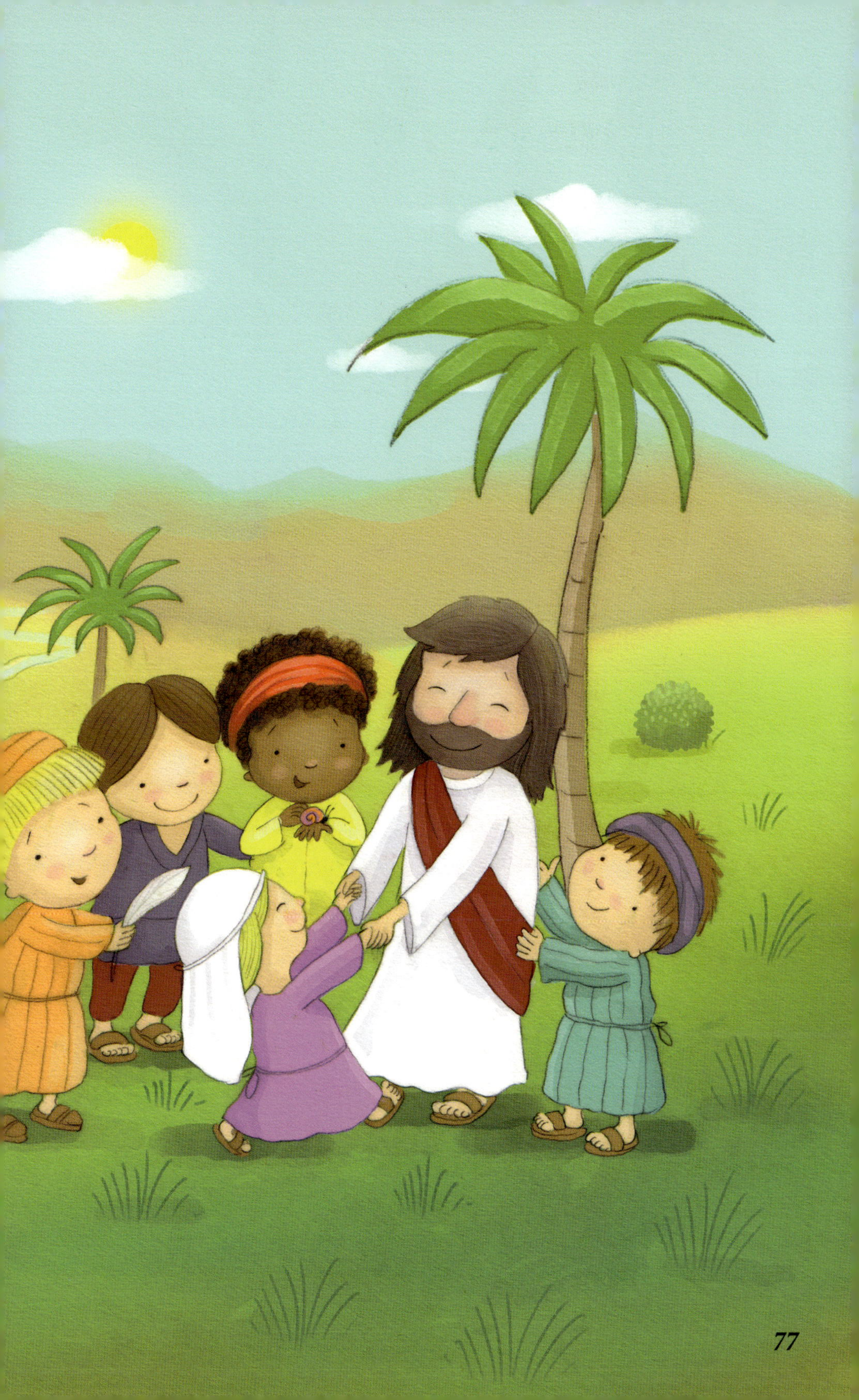

Zacchaeus is Changed

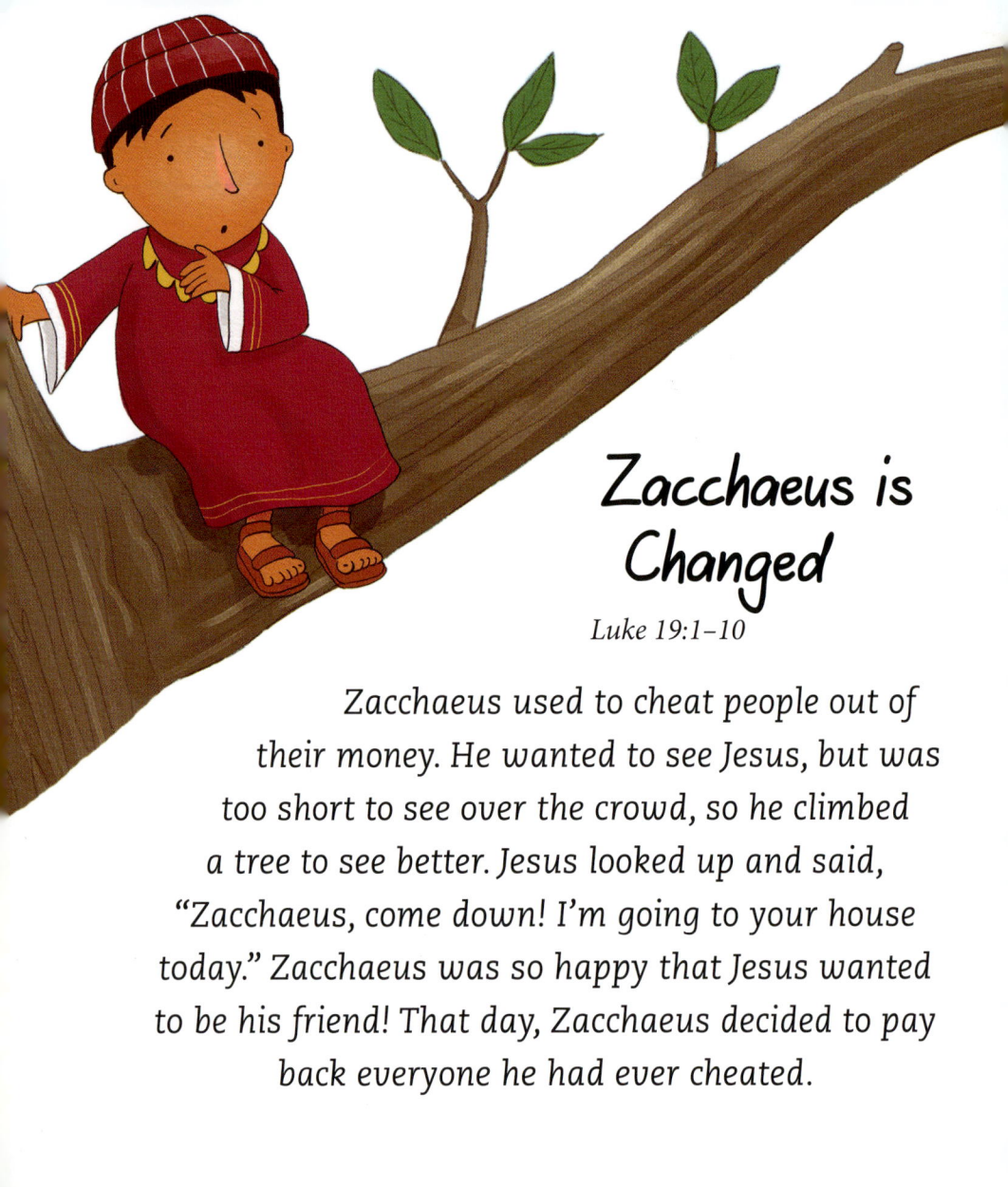

Luke 19:1–10

Zacchaeus used to cheat people out of their money. He wanted to see Jesus, but was too short to see over the crowd, so he climbed a tree to see better. Jesus looked up and said, "Zacchaeus, come down! I'm going to your house today." Zacchaeus was so happy that Jesus wanted to be his friend! That day, Zacchaeus decided to pay back everyone he had ever cheated.

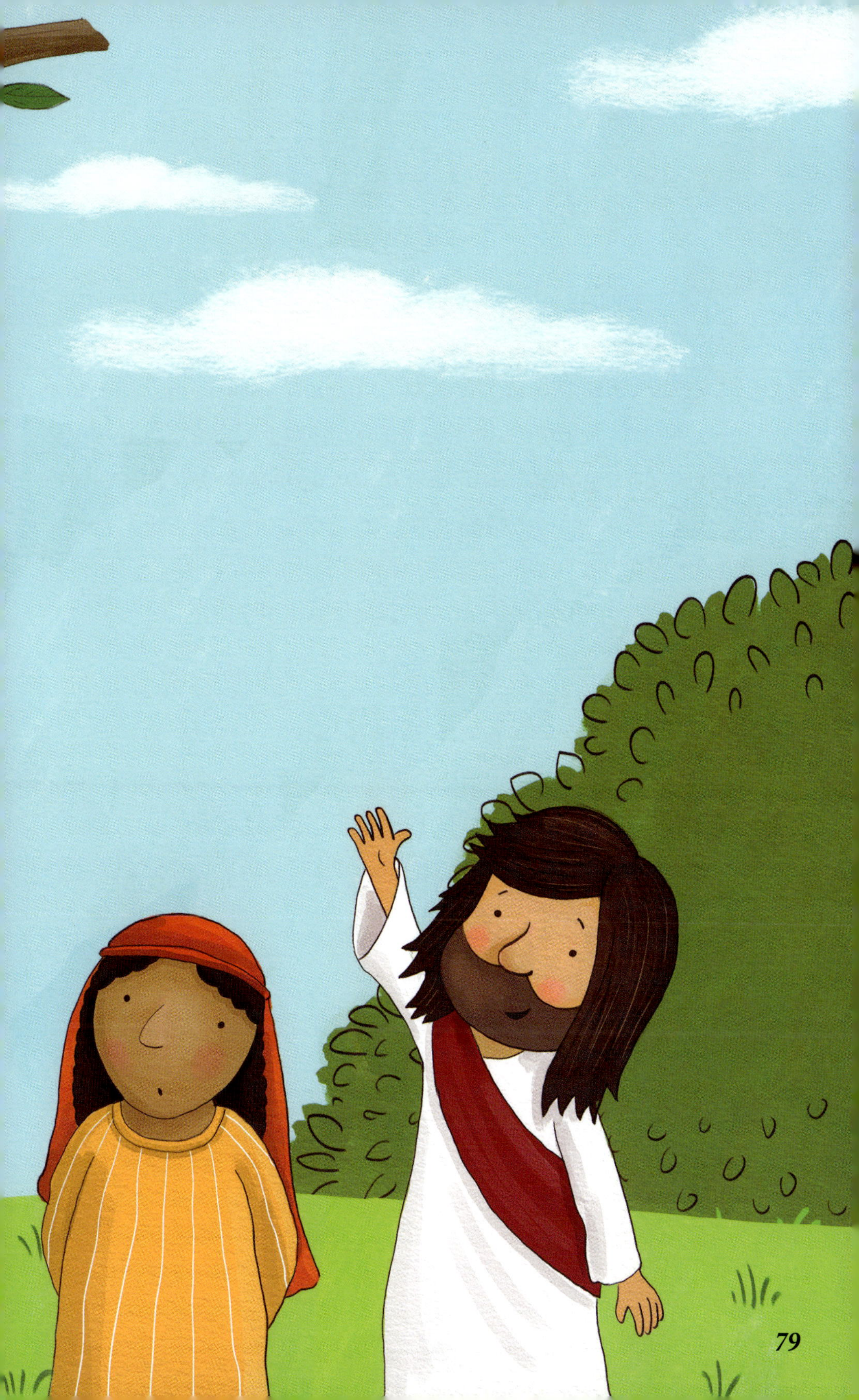

Jesus Rides into Jerusalem

Luke 19:28–44; John 12:12–19

Jesus was on His way to Jerusalem, and His followers found a donkey for Him to ride on. Everyone along the road started shouting, "Blessed is he who comes in the name of the Lord!" They laid cloaks and palm branches down in the road. Everyone was so excited to see Jesus! But some of the city leaders hated Jesus and wanted Him gone; they started planning ways to get rid of Him.

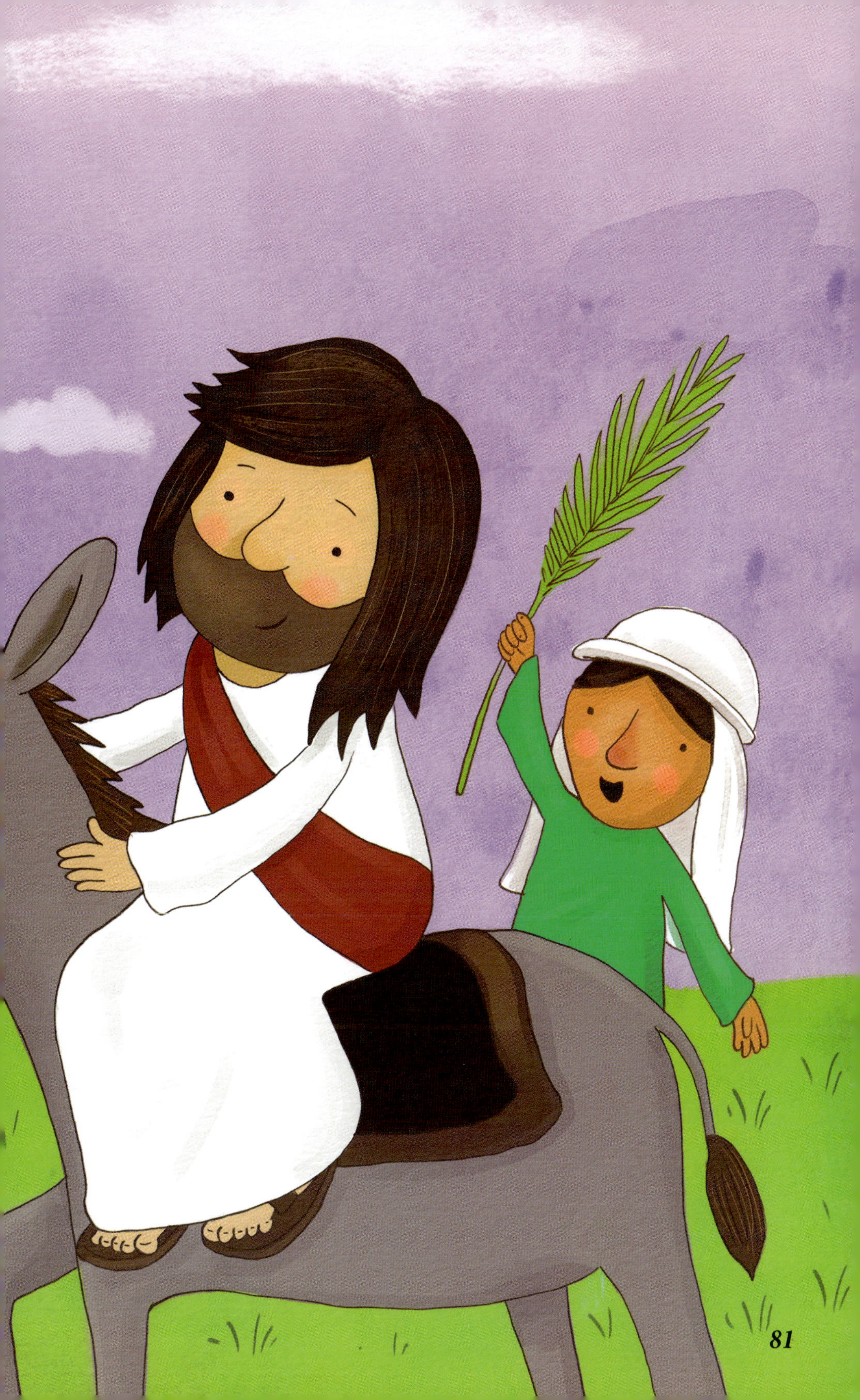

The Praise of Children

Matthew 21:14–17

When Jesus came to Jerusalem, the children kept shouting, "Hosanna to the Son of David!" Some of the religious leaders complained to Jesus about what the children were saying. Jesus quoted a psalm, reminding them that it said, "Lord, you have caused the lips of babies and young children to call out your praise."

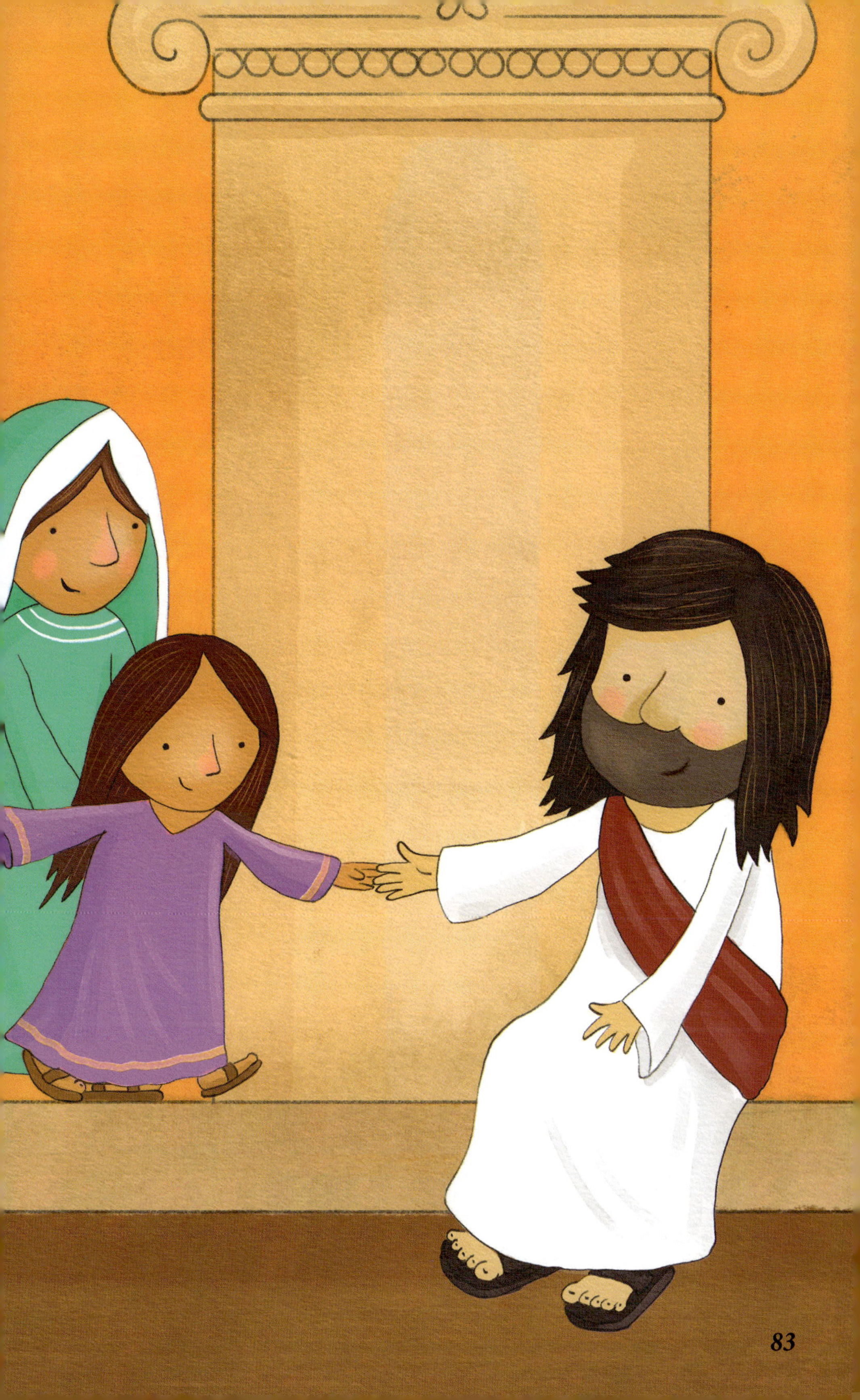

Jesus Dies on a Cross

Matthew 27:38-54; John 19:18,28-30

The jealous religious leaders arrested Jesus and convinced the governor to have Him executed. The soldiers whipped Jesus and hung Him on a cross. The people who had sung His praises a few days before now mocked Jesus and spit on Him. After several hours, Jesus died. The earth quaked when He died, and the soldiers said, "He really must have been the Son of God!"

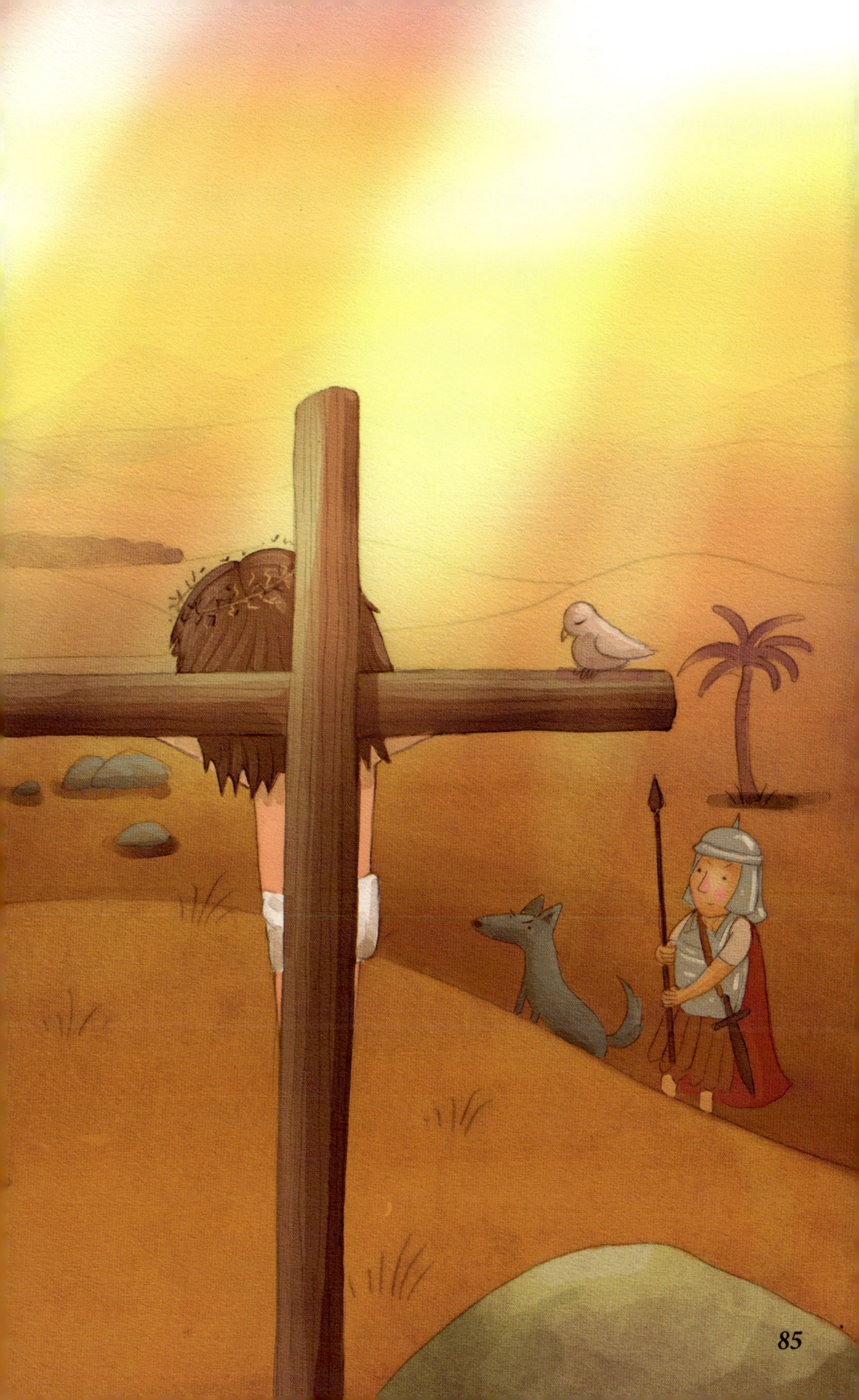

Jesus is Buried

Matthew 27:55–66; John 19:38–42

One of Jesus' followers made sure to bury Jesus in a tomb. The governor sent soldiers to guard the tomb, and they put a huge stone over the entrance. All of Jesus' followers and friends went home. They were very sad and shocked—Jesus was their Lord and Saviour, but now He was dead!

87

Jesus Defeats Death

Luke 24; John 20

Three days after Jesus died, some of His followers were on their way to His tomb. When they got there, the huge stone was rolled away, and His body was gone. Two angels appeared to them and said, "Jesus is not here. He has risen!" After that, Jesus appeared to them Himself—He was alive!

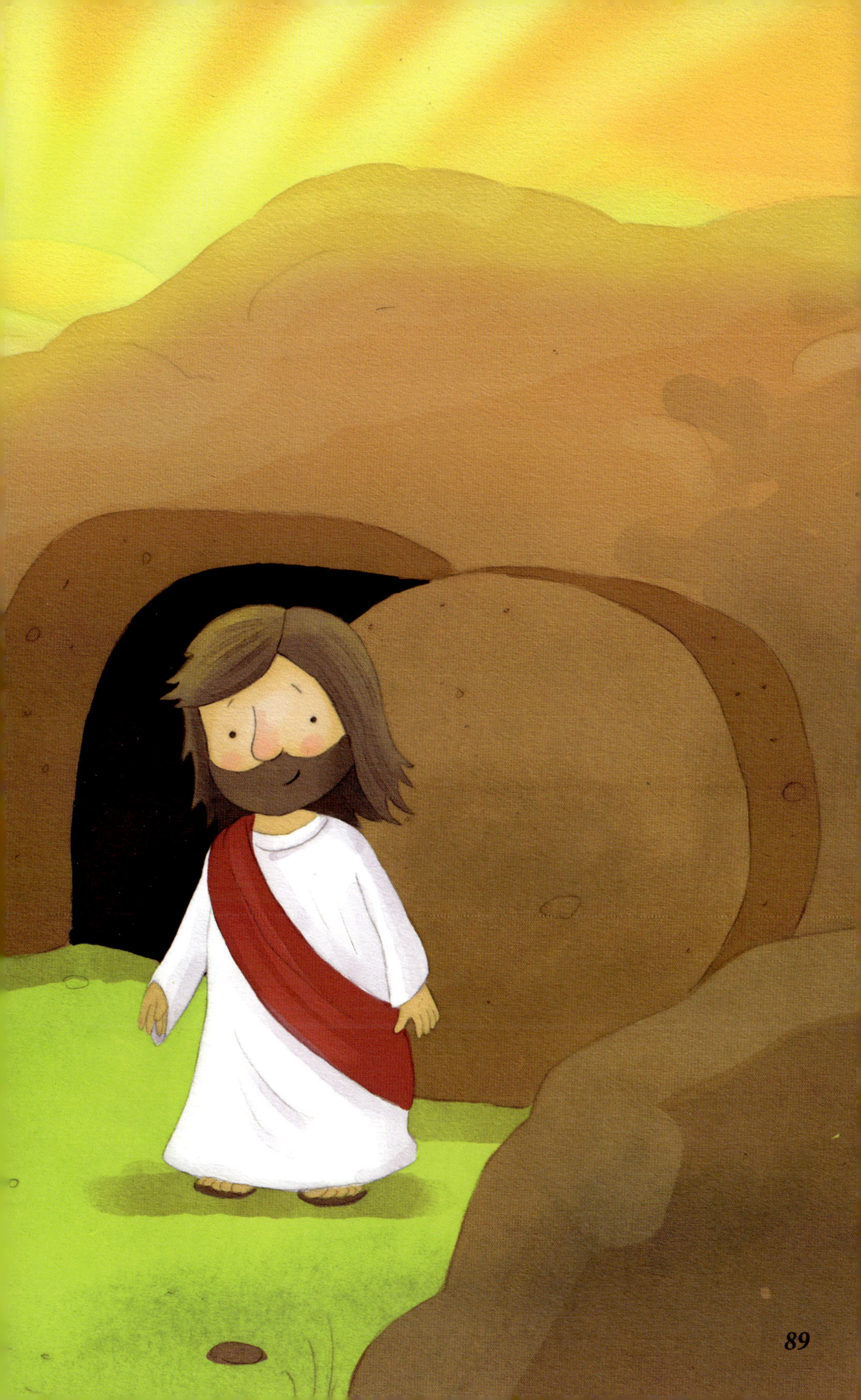

"I am with You Always!"

Matthew 28:16–20

Jesus met His followers in Galilee and spoke to them again. He told them to tell everyone about Him, and to teach new believers everything He had taught them. "I am with you always," He promised, "even until the end of the world!"

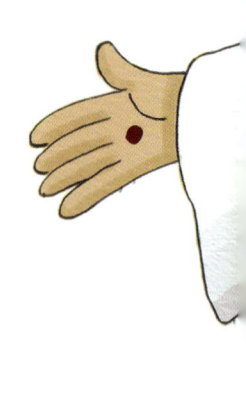

Jesus Returns to Heaven

Mark 16:19; Luke 24:50-51

After Jesus had said these things, He blessed His friends. While He was blessing them, He went up into heaven to be with His Father. Jesus' followers stared up in the sky where He had disappeared, but an Angel came to them and said, "Why are you standing around? Jesus will come back someday."

God's Great Salvation Plan

Ephesians 1:3–14

God chose us from the very beginning to be His children because He loves us. Sin separated us from God, but Jesus came to bring us back through His death and resurrection. He paid the price for all our sin and rose again to defeat death. When we believe that Jesus is God's son who came to save us, Jesus' blood washes away all of our sin so that we can be God's children and live with Him for ever.